MUSICAL SELECTIONS
in
"NEW YORK, NEW YORK"

Book Design © 1977
The Big 3 Music Corporation
New York, New York
Made in U.S.A. All Rights Reserved
International Copyright Secured

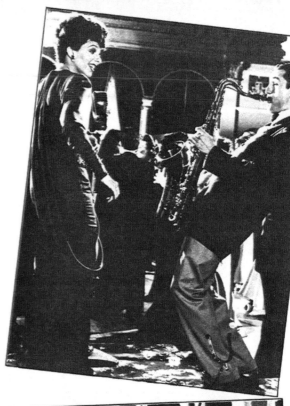

From the UNITED ARTISTS Motion Picture ''NEW YORK, NEW YORK''

THEME FROM NEW YORK, NEW YORK

Words by
FRED EBB

Music by
JOHN KANDER

3178

6

sleep ... to find I'm king of the hill, ___ top of the heap. My lit-tle town blues are melt-ing a-way, I'll make a brand new start ___ of it in old New

3178

York.

If I can make it there, ___ I'd make it

an - y - where, ___ It's up to you, New York, New

York.

king of the hill, head of the list, cream of the crop at the top of the heap.

From the UNITED ARTISTS Motion Picture ''NEW YORK, NEW YORK''

THERE GOES THE BALL GAME

Words by
FRED EBB

Music by
JOHN KANDER

3178

From the UNITED ARTISTS Motion Picture "NEW YORK, NEW YORK"

BUT THE WORLD GOES 'ROUND

Words by
FRED EBB

Music by
JOHN KANDER

3178

From the UNITED ARTISTS Motion Picture "NEW YORK, NEW YORK"

HAPPY ENDINGS

Words by
FRED EBB

Music by
JOHN KANDER

3178

the life I lead is less dra-mat-ic not re-mote-ly cin-e-mat-ic, Hap-py End-ings far as I can see are on-ly for the stars, not in the stars for me. me.

rit. e dim.

From the UNITED ARTISTS Motion Picture "NEW YORK, NEW YORK"

A NEW KIND OF LOVE

Words and Music by
SAMMY FAIN
IRVING KAHAL
PIERRE NORMAN

3178

From the UNITED ARTISTS Motion Picture "NEW YORK, NEW YORK"

ONCE IN A WHILE

Words by
BUD GREEN

Music by
MICHAEL EDWARDS

3178

From the UNITED ARTISTS Motion Picture "NEW YORK, NEW YORK"

YOU ARE MY LUCKY STAR

Words by
ARTHUR FREED

Music by
NACIO HERB BROWN

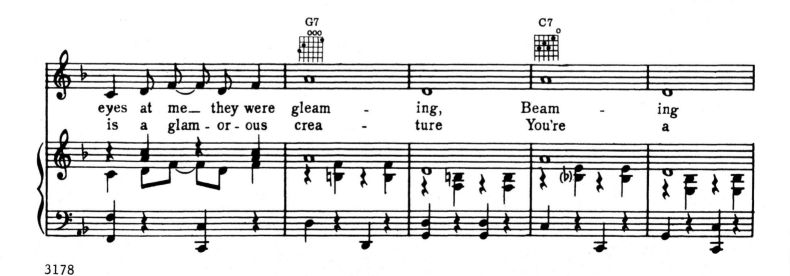

3178

From the UNITED ARTISTS Motion Picture "NEW YORK, NEW YORK"

IT'S A WONDERFUL WORLD

Lyric by
HAROLD ADAMSON

Music by
JAN SAVITT
JOHNNY WATSON

3178

Never, nev-er knew a bet-ter day _____ I've got

no kick com-ing ____ And I feel like hum-ming.

Chorus, Slow *(With feeling)*

It's A Won-der-ful World

I'm just walk-ing on air ____ Talk of heav-en on

3178

From the UNITED ARTISTS Motion Picture "NEW YORK, NEW YORK"

THE MAN I LOVE

Words by
IRA GERSHWIN

Music by
GEORGE GERSHWIN

3178

REFRAIN

3178

From the UNITED ARTISTS Motion Picture "NEW YORK, NEW YORK"

JUST YOU, JUST ME

Lyric by
RAYMOND KLAGES

Music by
JESSE GREER

From the UNITED ARTISTS Motion Picture ''NEW YORK, NEW YORK''

DON'T BE THAT WAY

Words and Music by
BENNY GOODMAN
EDGAR SAMPSON
MITCHELL PARISH

3178

37

From the UNITED ARTISTS Motion Picture "NEW YORK, NEW YORK"

BLUE MOON

Lyric by
LORENZ HART

Music by
RICHARD RODGERS

From the UNITED ARTISTS Motion Picture "NEW YORK, NEW YORK"

HONEYSUCKLE ROSE

Words by
ANDY RAZAF

Music by
THOMAS WALLER

From the UNITED ARTISTS Motion Picture "NEW YORK, NEW YORK"

DON'T GET AROUND MUCH ANYMORE

Lyric by
BOB RUSSELL

Music by
DUKE ELLINGTON

3178

From the UNITED ARTISTS Motion Picture "NEW YORK, NEW YORK"

DO NOTHIN' TILL YOU HEAR FROM ME

Lyric by
BOB RUSSELL

Music by
DUKE ELLINGTON

3178

From the UNITED ARTISTS Motion Picture "NEW YORK, NEW YORK"

TAKING A CHANCE ON LOVE

Lyrics by
JOHN LATOUCHE
TED FETTER

Music by
VERNON DUKE

3178